# Fair Su~

## SUSAN BARBA

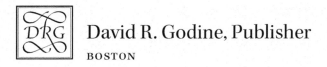 David R. Godine, Publisher

BOSTON

First published in 2017 by
DAVID R. GODINE, PUBLISHER
Post Office Box 450
Jaffrey, New Hampshire 03452
*www.godine.com*

LIBRARY OF CONGRESS CATALOGING-IN-PUBLICATION DATA
Names: Barba, Susan, author.
Title: Fair sun / by Susan Barba.
Description: Jaffrey, New Hampshire : David R. Godine,
    Publisher, [2017] | Includes bibliographical references.
Identifiers: LCCN 2016050099| ISBN 9781567926019 (acid-free
    paper) | ISBN 1567926010 (acid-free paper)
Classification: LCC PS3602.A755 A6 2017 | DDC 811/.6—dc23
LC record available at https://lccn.loc.gov/2016050099

SECOND PRINTING, 2017
*Printed in the United States of America*

# Fair Sun

*For my mother, Susan Vartanian Barba,*
*and in memory of my father, J. William Barba*

# Contents

I.

13   In the Shadows

14   To Know Wisdom and Instruction

15   Yerevan—New York—Yerevan—New York

17   Diptych

18   Seeking Even the Smallest of Signs

20   Le Palais Idéal

21   The Color of Nostalgia

22   Arrangements for Departure

23   How Things Speak then Pass

24   Convalescence

26   The Social Graces

27   Attachment

28   To Abbazia di Novacella

30   Fair Sun

33   Look Out for Hope


II.

37   Andranik


III.

49   Requiem for the Stars

50   Where the Lone Clarity?

53   Sketch

54   Failed Sublime

55   Elective Affinities

56   Night Painting

57   Christina, Dancing

58   How Should We Live Our Lives?

59   Summer Birth

60   No Explanation

61   Dyer Pond

62   From the Outermost Island

64 Inverted Pendulum

65 Bread and Flowers

66 A Year in New England

68 Interior

70 This Republic

71 Nowhere

72 At the A.R.T.

74 Reverie

76 Talking Cure

78 Liminal

79 Gammon

80 Marathon

81 The Forest Next Door

83 *Acknowledgments*

85 *Notes*

*Aravod luso, aregakn ardar…*     First light, fair sun …

NERSES SHNORHALI, from *The Book of Hours*


Why is the sun fair?

Because it shines down equally on everyone.

ANDRANIK VARTANIAN, in conversation

I.

# In the Shadows

Places a child never wants to go,
under the mulberries whose black juice stains the soles,
beneath the windbreak of cedars shedding their bark
in shreds, the same brown as the dead cicadas.
Squat on the hill, the incinerator of detritus,
compacted of leaves, bracken, last summer's weeds.
And higher, the gated garden, the rusted latch
requiring full weight shouldered against the door
before the bolt would budge and shudder,
and the door bump open, catching on tufts of grass.
In the solar system of the child,
the garden would be the sun. In her nightly prayer,
with mother, father, safe from harm.
How close they are to one another,
the garden, the fire pit, the dark groves,
a panting dash by day, hair's breadth by night,
the golden orbs of apricots,
the darkness of the dirt that feeds them.

# To Know Wisdom and Instruction

Her first word
    careful
taught the girl
    of care
and danger
    in the world
how words
    contain
the menace
    and the knowledge
years had
    yet to reach.

# Yerevan—New York—Yerevan—New York

What to do with the five flies
grazing this head of cheese?
Or the texture of this carpet's blue,
which is the weight of water
on a cloudy day at Sevan Lake,
and the pattern of fish, of dragons,
weaving the drowned and mythic
together—what will save them?

If not language, then a currency?
Something hard that answers
the cry at the marketplace?
"Why, if you say how beautiful
don't you buy it?" Own it
and your tongue fumbles
for coins in the dark change purse
of your mouth.

\*

In a sketch by Dalí
it's a closer look brings you
eye to eye with a skull—
two larger grapes toward the cluster's
stem forming sockets of the absent
eyes. In the bone-clean room
of the museum, two grapes grow
glaucous with a powdery bloom
of ripeness, rounding
with the pleasure of a riddle.

\*

Somewhere green, a man
tucks with a shepherd's crook
a tendril into the woven roof
of grapevines outside his door.
Neighboring, I watch—

But he stands in the dappled
suns of his living roof,
holding his crozier,
wearing a cape of light.

*


A man is pouring water from a pail.
A man is speaking as though pouring
water from a pail.
He is too far for me to understand him,
his meaning flashing and reflecting,
a shadow tossed by the sun
back at me. But I recognize the sound
of the rushing, the mass of it hitting
the ground, the bright white sound of it.

# Diptych

*after Arshile Gorky*

Sometimes dead bees and other times blossoms. A room's set fire by
laughter, resplendent, leaping headlong in asthmatic grandeur. I cover
my ears to hear it flowing. Outside, it would be red and bold and one
must bow to it. Bent over the knee, watching the inside flow out.

This life in which the child protects the mother. In which he stands with
velvet collar and flower in hand, and his mother, made impassive, is a
horizon. She is a Rothko painting and he is the inquiry. She is a well that
swallows his pennies silently. She is a swallow. The winged movements
he traces.

# Seeking Even the Smallest of Signs

First they pulled from the burning a miracle, then a mistake.
The Lord will lift them the priest with the grief
in his eyes cried. Lord, what blue eyes bound there,
what hurling, diving, shining, burning—
reason surfaces and sinks, sinks and surfaces.

Dawn without sunrise. Gray. Purple.
Her Majesty in mourning. Her Majesty the warring. In the double
house of life all this was repeating itself,
*Naneferkaptah had already himself lived Setne's story.*

When the rains began the teams with two-by-fours
found the going treacherous as those in the desert found
the food wretched. They prayed to the golden serpent on the staff
to save them. And the serpent stretched itself
    tap, tap
and became a hymn, white-throated, rising to give
itself up for the good of the chosen ones.

    Mother I remember the buttons on your dressing gown.
    So blue and beady-eyed and true, when did I begin

To fear them. The world now
not so round with us. Velocity
threatening to meet, to marry
density at every corner
    carrying
    carrying

Who can see
        the writing on our foreheads almost wet still
Who can see
        tap, tap

        algae bloom beneath the board
        smoke from the sky

Tell me if that is a hand
if it is human what
will it
speak

## Le Palais Idéal

To report the weather well requires
not just accuracy but empathy.

Tonight, not just clear but a moonlit sky,
and already we're dreaming.

From pebbles on the road, a palace built,
and tiredness forgotten, the daily route,

not rote but purposeful. So the artist
hoards his pebbles, tumbles and thumbs them,

treasures, not loose change. Nothing useless,
even a holiday, person, town will leave

something to be pressed between the pages,
dried but undiminished. Temporary

no more the saddest word. The postman Cheval's
palace gave him peace and proof of days.

Some say the greater peace may come from knowing
the palace too will pass. Such predictions

leave me cold. Give me the bolt of blue
Nvart Vartanian cut, pieced, and stitched

into a dress her daughter wore and I
now wear, her sense of proportion, her nimble hand.

# The Color of Nostalgia

A boy I knew once said my childhood
reminded him of the last idyll of the Russian empire,
the nineteenth-century days of Nicholas II,
before Rasputin, before the revolution.

And he was right, though I hadn't known it then—
candlelight flickering in the arched dining room windows,
handmade lace dresses, bows in our long hair,
quince and peaches from the orchard in the summer,

ironed sheets and ironed underwear.
How rich we were as children to live there
in the old world in New Jersey with the adults
who were both landowners and serfs,

Papa sweating in the garden heaped with watermelons,
Daddy clearing the woods of underbrush,
Medzi smocking dresses, canning tomatoes,
and Mom, more beautiful than Empress Alexandra, ironing, ironing.

The land around us, oaks and maples, enlarged
the days reflected back to us, serene.
The day that Daddy left for the city, waiting by the garage
for a hug I answered with a wave

the idyll ended, taking him then Medzi, Papa too.
Giants of the earth all gone. In the poverty of the present,
the land is under snow, late afternoon light
turning the shadows blue. Something moves in my field

of vision. It is a fox picking his way like a dancer
from trunk to trunk, his coat the color of the dead unfallen
oak leaves, a rust one shade darker
than the grasses in the unmown fields.

# Arrangements for Departure

[ flight or fight]
A feeling beneath the right breast. Questions in the head but in the torso a distinct feeling not of numbness. When the paperweight fell it hit hard and rolled. Coming into the room she knew someone had been there and was gone. How fast the dusk fell so that the winter sun had barely warmed her skin before she had to pull the blanket up. One then three then two again. Watch how he sweeps the knight up to replace him, as if turning a doorknob. Tick. Tock. There stands a king now. The square is never empty. Always grey, or gray, depending on whom you're with. Leave it. Quickly.

[alight]
Pomegranates everywhere you turn now. Less so with terebinth, though oranges and coffee yet. The birds and the bears. Hand in hand in hand. Hikmet said, what sort of business is this brothers? Only hand in hand remaining. An empty palm. A line that splits but continues to a number unforeseen. How many more heartbeats, footsteps, blinks of the eyes. Soon no one else will know what we have known.

[song to myself]
Today is fine. Tomorrow it will rain.

[laughter]
Silver bells of the Latin alphabet and seismic rumblings in all the languages of the world.

[raft]
I want to leave unnoticed while my house lies at peace. Down the stairs in love and in silence, to leave the darkened rooms whose hallways are lit again in dreams.

# How Things Speak Then Pass

*after Andrei Tarkovsky*

Before the boy's heart he holds a milk bottle, white in the twilight
    as a lantern,
larger than his hands, his head, his shadow larger
than his frame and dark, except for the milk in its mother of pearl
body. Almost too heavy to hold, the bottle tips and
spills into his mouth. God it is good, this cold, this glass
lip against soft lip, slipping in and sinking
like fishing line from the tilt of hands down to the belly.

Not as a sound exists, waning unseen, but as the hourglass,
how the sand poured smooth, legions aligning to slip
escape to lower regions, leaving the upper bulb clear and clean
through which we saw Olya blooming against the opposite wall.
Time to go dancing, she'd say and in her belly the small creature stirring
like her turning in her sleep toward the owl's questions the night sends
him to ask, the white handiwork at the windows billowing—

# Convalescence

The white corners of the cape hover
overhead,

the air folded into angles,
creased.

Fever makes the skin over skull feel
softer.

A ripe stone fruit in an envelope.

An arm has come untucked,

a woman's freckled arm

my own.

As a girl I loved that given
crook of inner elbow
in which my chin
or cheek or brow
could burrow,
a perfect fit,
like coming home.

Children memorize
        then grow out of
themselves

into other arms

into Life
its capital vistas

Outside the grasses swaying green and greener,
and the high shine of cicadas.

Muted, aquarial, the light
slides along the origami walls,
the cyclops-octopus in bed.

I watch the painting opposite

giant canvas describing fog
and a small house in sunlight near the edge

by afternoon what was all subject
now is surface, texture,
unpigmented impasto

even the air
thick with atoms
tonic.

# The Social Graces

On her hands and knees sometimes
she finds
          a barrette

all else—the extra yardage
          plumes the color of her dresses costume jewelry
                    bundled to the girl next door

          such butterflies
                    her girls

          who could've pinned them then

          then wallflowers just out of season

                    unregarded, waiting to be dismissed

how white-haired charity remembers
          wanders the garden

spooning compote meditating

          the decomposing trampoline
          absent cries
          even the dogs led down this avenue unseen

forbearance

          their father in pinstripes unfailingly

at the door no more

          the neighbors come and go in vehicles.

# Attachment

What if dance had never married music?
Movement free of measure, free of time,

how sometimes sun reflecting off the water
brings to mind a music of its own.

*In broad daylight even the sounds*, Fernando
said, *must shine*, and *I have wanted so*

*like sounds to live by things and not be theirs*,
to circulate as gift or mendicant,

or failing that at least to see these trees,
dispassionate and pliant, without envy,

bending, bending, bending as a body
bends and does not break but bears itself

with grace or energy or weariness,
alone unlike the trees in unison.

What troupe of dancers has the unity
of trees, what music the dispatch of wind?

## To Abbazia di Novacella

Begin walking and the mind starts

turning the wind drifts smelling of apple

and larch and lower of heat in the grasses.

Blue blazes mark the path feet follow

thoughts furrow in the sloped orchard

lift across the valley to the train

carrying what along its track of action

linear along the range the sun

in local stone chiseled here

above a door and so in Rome

in Anatolia in Armenia,

eternity contained within a star.


In the chapel I join the line

to the altar one thought held in mind

as the wafer's held in mouth.

As a child I heard my father

cry out having closed his teeth on it

pained like I'd not seen before

not by nerve endings but by faith

in the wounding of flesh not his

released in a yelp of regret.

I hadn't known till then to stem

reflex, accepting communion

like a snack.


Silence the muscles of the mouth

the working jaw stop

speaking and the world starts

speaking to one sudden as

salt on the tongue.

# Fair Sun

One by one
    they are going.

Everyone the sun
    shone down on,

everyone the earth grew,
    watered, fed, and rooted.

Often they're gone at once
    in a historic storm.

In my life it has been slow
    but sure

as drops from a gutter,
    and unlike water drying,

dripping faster now.
    The sun cannot come out

and slow it to a stop.
    This morning I was

at an airport
    trying to get from Chappaquidick

back to town.
    The man behind the desk

knew of no flights.
    He offered me his car

and reaching for his keys, shuffled
        some photos into view—

kids at the beach, I recognized
        myself! My mother young as me now,

my father, alive, and rising
        from the water,

my name in his throat,
        drops caught shining

in his small nest of chest hairs,
        and I am snorting water

like my daughter at the pond,
        and freckled, and it's the present still,

the kind, astonished man behind the desk,
        my current haste,

and the man to my left I see
        is my father's brother, and we are

riding the waves,
        so buoyant that I wake.

Restored. To carry
        the feeling in my body

a little longer
        please.

To place it in the scales
     against the weight that is

the friend coming home
     this week for hospice.

The lightness at the windows
     eats away at the lightness

inside, as things with mass
     begin to push

all those without
     away.

Restored,
     remember.

No balance
     but to repeat

the feeling, being alive
     under the same sun once

into this day, which will be overcast
     I see,

the sun invisible for now,
     above us all the same.

# Look Out for Hope

*after Robert Frank*

A cold bronze horse,
foreleg lifted
to paw at snow
or soda cans below
as wind and sun
sweep bare its form
that takes up space.

Round the horse
the seasons spin
to wither on the plinth
where students gather
and forget everything
the head can hold,
spilled by laughing
and a looseness
in their limbs.

But that boy leaning,
talking with
his hands and thin
under the wool,
his face like someone
you once knew—
he'd look away
if smiled at, too often
he forgets the fact
of arms and legs,
believing the mind
a whistling reed,
turned by a lathe
with intent.

II.

# Andranik

Papa, what happened before the burning barn? What happened when you were at your house? Did your father come back to find you?

Oh, my father. Well, you know. When they start killing, my father that night came. That night came. And see we were all gathered in the big house. In our house. They had seen there, is empty. So he came. Talked to me. He say, I take you. We go to Honey River side. Hide us in the bush. So. He took me. I have a dog. And the dog followed us. And just edge the river. River. Is thick. Some kind of bamboo. Hide ourself there. My father and me. So. After the gendarmerie on horseback. They. Hundreds run all around. Find to kill. To rob. They come close to us where my father and me hiding and our dog with us. When gendarmerie come our dog bark, run after the horses. Oh gendarmerie find this hiding thing. They come.

They took your father then?

They caught my father.

What did they do to your father?

I throw. I throw myself.

What did they do to your father, Papa?

They killed.

Right there? In front of you?

My father only have a dagger. He didn't have a gun. They caught my father. My father was a big man, over six feet, a strong man. And three, four Kurds, dagger and gun. They didn't shoot. They say the bullet is worth more than the man. So my father tried to get the Turkish, Kurdish gun. But one Kurd hit my father right here. And my father whispering throw yourself in the water. I throw myself in the water. I was a very good swimmer because every day summer I used to swim the deep. So I swim far away. And the Kurds they took my father's clothing. Nothing left on. And they gone.

What did you do with your father?

My. You know. Next. Yet it was not quite light. I went. They had took my
father's clothing. Nothing was left on him.

And his watch?

And. Ants. You know they like. I pull my father's. You know. Was far away
the water and the river. Honey River. Is sweet water and soft yellow sand.
I pulled my father close to the water and with hands I dig the sand and
I rolled my father in and covered with sand.

Tell about your sister.

My sister Gohareeg. She look like you. She had been very beautiful.
Beautiful. They called, you know, the Kurds, far away.

Did they take her? What happened? What happened to her?

They. She had. Kurds. Mahmoudoh name had take her. So. They had.
After escaped. She had run. Throw herself in river. Honey River. Deep
river. Killed herself. River. So.

About two days walking reached a village.

Did you have any water or food when you were walking?

No. No. And no water. They drive us far away from where the water or thing. No body. And some this woman got a little, I see, walking, a lady have a little boy. Baby. Other says, "*Kouyrig*, please when he peeps let I have it." She says, "Oh *kouyrig*, it's second day I haven't had one drop of water." And I see she is feeding the child. Is dry. Is crying. See. So. They took us and that evening put us in a great big barn. Like you know, like getting fish and putting in a barrel. In a barrel. So. I was fortunate. Pushing. Pushing. Pushing. Reached to the wall. I see a hole there. Wall. The villager had opened the wall. Summertime they dry the things. When they put hay not to be moldy. I slipped out from there.

That's how you were able to escape.

I slipped out. About from here to go as far as to Cherrillo's house. There was a ditch. I dumped in. In mud and bamboos. From there other boys come. Some they caught. Gendarmeries caught. Pour gasoline and match. Burn. So. I was very good knowing how to go toward the mountains. And before. You know. All the time the teacher said, "Boys, girls, you have got to know your country like your five fingers in front of your eye. Front of your eye. Sometime that will save your life." So. I hide myself in the bamboos and ditch. When it started dark I started going toward the mountains.

So Kurds when have come. The Kurds one down there. Talks there. He wants to go around. Puts feet just rock over Belouz's feet. He had pulled Belouz out. And there hatchet.

Hatchet?

Long-handled. Wooden-handled and here is like this. Sharp. To cut wood. To cut things. And had hit Belouz here. Cut ribs. The things. But not dead. Oh Belouz was. "I am burning." Was not dead. Ribs. What. "I am burning. Please one drop of water. One drop of water. *Mek gateel joor, mek gateel joor g'khentrem.*" And I can't go. After when all the Kurds gone. I have a hat. Handmade like tapestry is made. Good hat. I went. Fulled the water. Water was running. I put. I took to Belouz. He drink. "Oh, *khosh.*" After until midnight. He cried and cried. Died. And next morning, I decided to be dead. Not to hide myself. I didn't hide myself.

Papa, when you were sent into the barn to get the jewelry and things, were there any children?

Oh, see. When I gave myself to Kurds. Turks. The Turks they gathered us to search the houses and burning barns and corpse. Before they had gold bracelets, things. That house I was searching, the Turks were sitting in high things there and drinking arak. They decide if that day we had not found anything they were going to kill us. The old women and me. So I see far, you know, that barn. Barn. An old lady standing. Dead. Choked to death in the burning barn. The burning things, the wooden beams fallen so she had not fallen this way, just back towards wall and standing like alive. Alive. So, the Armenian have a habit of very nice made thing like that. Apron. Apron. I see this woman standing, in back is a wall and timber had fallen so that she had not fallen this way. Is there. So, I went to her. I went to her. I lifted the apron. I see a little girl like here. A golden thing here. Pieces. And silver top and golden thing here, golden here. Golden here. See, I took to gendarmeries. Oh, gendarmeries so happy and they decide not to kill me. So. After. Next day they killed some of the women.

See, there were cruel things that Turks had organized. Have happened when I had given up myself winter to that Kurdish house. They need me because I take care, sweeping. Oh, so hard work for me. But I have enough to eat.

And, and have happened that house I were in one Kurdish. Kurdish, you know, mullah, preacher. Had come to that house. That house where I was, was chief's house. They make him shish kebab, things. Eat and wash beard, hands, and so on. After eating so well, he say, "You know, any house I go to eat and make *nahmas*"—wash myself—"if that house there is *gavoor*"—unbeliever, the Christians are *gavoor*, infidels—"that's *haram*. It is not clean for me if I eat there. So got to be killed. Killed."

So, my *agha* took my ear, brought me to him. "This I've got at my house." So others they brought others. About a dozen like myself age boys. One, my playmate. We had been together when we were crawling and studying. Torkom name. Torkom.

And have happened that Torkom's mother when pregnant to give birth, my mother be pregnant unfortunately to give birth to me. And they summertime, the women come. Sit. Throw mats. Sit and tell stories. And Torkom's mother and my mother said, "*Kouyrig*," they are pregnant, they say, "If one be a boy, one be a girl, they marry together." See they make. Unfortunately my mother gives birth to me and Torkom's mother gives boy. And we grow together.

Like brothers. Yes, all the time together.

Day and night. Summer outside we sleep on mats. Moon. Stars. And daytime go swim and chase ducks.

So happened that after months when I escaped from the burning barn and went to the mountains they brought him. After it was winter.

And what happened?

I killed Torkom.

How?

They, you know, the mullah when he eat shish kebab, everything. They say. So. They want to make fun. Play. They put two guns to the wall. In one gun, live bullet. In one gun, no bullet. No live bullet. Like me and Torkom there. Guns into wall. They say, "Go get a gun." I went. Torkom. We went together. I lift a gun. Torkom lift a gun. See. I didn't know if the gun there is a live bullet or no. Torkom didn't know. So. About twelve feet far from each other. And. And ordered, shoot. I shoot and killed Torkom. My gun have live bullet. I killed him.

So. They. They make enjoy.

See.
That's a cruel human being.

III.

# Requiem for the Stars

*after Mallarmé*

Black hole, where the stars go when they die,
no region of my brain illuminates
your name. Black hole, the circuitry
goes dark, fumbling for metaphors to grasp
how gravity absorbs a galaxy.
Except the white page and its hieroglyphic
scars, the stars of black ink drunken by
the sheet, white sheet magnetic in its pull,
absorbing finished thoughts that end in words.
O words, without you what would be the last?
And what would last? A void, an endless night
whose mother is that galaxy of time;
the milky way, our astral address,
ephemeral as the imprint of a kiss.

# Where the Lone Clarity?

Take off your old
words

this is the New Economy.

       The moon so bright the waters luciferous.

What should we sing?
Should we sing of systems?

You cup your hands—
the world.

Return potential still attractive.

       On the other side the rising darkly.

The problem of doubt.
The problem of visibility.


\*

       I lost my shadow
       somewhere in this city
          or on the lawn
            it loosened, slipped

and I kept going.

\*


After they emigrated he sold fruit meat

held up and shot on Christmas Eve

and lived

repeating

*still alive*

repeating

*Nani, what I seen, what I seen*

\*

Where can I look
to find my shadow?

       Many streets now where I would not could not

others gone from them
      hunched in their glowing tarps

O relief! rationed
            not from any lack of—

may it be sewn
          this mantle of complicity

fast


salvation through the eye of—

sees black/white.

But the static
        gray between

the changing weather we walk out into

# Sketch

Daughter, wife, mother, she is all three. She will not
be depicted.

High-heeled and flushed amid her brood,
not she.

Something about her
shuns adornment,
uneasy with life's
fecundity

and yet not fully nor without
regret that it should be.
Sometimes she wonders
at her sisters.

Down a sand road at dusk and heading for the winter beach,
waving the car back to the empty glowing house

she sees herself so clearly
at a distance.

# Failed Sublime

To float through purple rooms unencumbered,
yelling, singing to oneself, gulping
air and unafraid to take up space,
declare aloud a life. No order and

no fretting over disorder. No demurring
or changing in the dark, but feeling moonlight
the full length of the back, sunlight
on the belly. Lounging unslippered, clattering

down the stairs, ranging from wing to wing
of the house and flying—why else would shoulders ache?
Thrust open your chest, picture the hinged
appendages fissuring, feathering, our bones

heavy so the wingspan would be wider
than a bird's, no weightless cadence but
the heavy whomph of oiled wings. Close
your eyelids, sunspots burn against the black

ringed red, but there's no seeing in.
Your hands rest in your lap, cupped in each other's
clasp, the skin over loose tissue over
bone. How warm they are and not yet mottled.

Foreshortened torso, distant feet, your own.
Small of the back, distended shoulder, arms
with hands fastened, hair the fingers run through
on the head unseen, eyes known only

by reflection. When will it be face
to face and must it be outside our bodies?
Of salt is man, dissolute,
and of the earth, dreaming of blue-black wings.

# Elective Affinities

Your father said she's dying
out of order.

Against all odds you said
I'm still making
sentences in bed.

Now the ice melts with no one
to speak its ambition,
the faces in the boughs blossom
unseen, the fire hydrants
fail as artists.

Like us, you kept company
with yourself, but you (Susanna, Olga,
Svetlana, S. L. Boym) were manifold,
America your pet, a *wunderkammer*,
the setting for a play

you upstaged, leaving four books,
a yellow house on Shepard Street,
and lipstick traces on the tines,
biography dispersed by centrifugal force.

Here it's spring without the rites.
Apparatchiks are sliding in the slush,
and the authors are estranged.

Only uranium is as devoted
an alchemist as you. How were you
so unafraid of your own time?

# Night Painting

The infernal flicker of this city
gaslights strolling visitors,

tricks the river into thinking
its black ribbon is gem-embedded,

pearl lights, pale yolks, spilling skyward,
zygotes shivering in the waters.

The studio confirms this double
vision, attar of turpentine,

litany of chemical color,
spectral sight, as after sun.

Museum lawn of dew and cadmium,
Night and Day, the babies' heads,

giant domed dreaming sentries,
close- and open-lidded, twinned.

Emerald arborways unravel
homeward, the brick city not seen,

only ornate cornices, white
in the headlights, taillights red.

Morning, a dark chapel, brims,
amplified by bird cry.

Faint residue of the real,
pale watercolor wash.

# Christina, Dancing

Postmodern goddess,
    Veuve Clicquot
in hand
    and Nike feet,

queen at the prow,
    plowing the star-
lit sea,
    the tilting floor

tonight steers by
    your errant light,
intrinsic
    and reflected.

Numerous moons
    along the chartless
passage
    beyond ceremony,

the vessel peopled,
    singly or in pairs,
and proximate
    each other,

sometimes with cause
    to dance as now,
the deck
    beneath us, holding.

# How Should We Live Our Lives?

With love
and trepidation
sign our letters?

Conceive a child only
after much forethought
or none at all?

Follow the dialectical
heart to world's end
and feel it

tighten, a muscle,
to fill again,
unfettered? Daughter,

as you grow up I
will grow old,
a fact that shocks

you, even at age three.
Love has no part in this.
Only the sea

is free of such calculations,
and sometimes a person
too, running

into the sea in late summer when
the water remembers just barely
what it was to be cold.

# Summer Birth

I saw the end that night in late July,
out on the lawn, bearing the pulse of pain,
that pain no man will ever know, which rends
enclosure, and the light comes pouring through.
Such darkness it is women's charge to carry,
through winter nights and mornings dark as night,
a temporary dark so final-seeming,
it overwrites the memory of day.
How strange that life begins with this eclipse
of self, and sorrow of apartness. Animal—
I curled inside the winter-long and leaned
toward spring, till sun broke over Boston and
the fuse inched green through buds and leaves and bloomed.
So love will pick the petals and we let it.

# No Explanation

As children we played together
and by played I mean
we'd chant Christina sucks
until my sister, the youngest and the only other
girl, got red and shoved the next to youngest
in a snow bank where they'd try to stuff
each other's faces in the snow.

Now they are men,
and let me put it this way:
if you were walking down a road and one drove by,
he'd raise a hand in greeting,
all but him, the one most loved.
If he were at the wheel,
he wouldn't even see you,
he couldn't see you at all.

# Dyer Pond

Systole, diastole. To be alive
is almost always to be of two minds.
The Janus nature of the tide, the sea,
unable to be still, restless, compelled

(so like a woman!) by Lady Moon,
replete, then emptied. Driven thus,
despite the ocean's lulling pulse,
because the pulse reminds us of us,

we leave the beach, its present tense,
for more historic waters. My mother
slips her sandals off to feel the trail,
I follow barefoot, as I used to.

Deep in scrub oak, the kettle pond
brims. A thimbleful of time,
this dimple in the woods. September,
fall's molder, faint and high,

drifts by. The far bank
green stippled red. Soft silt,
warm water. Tea-colored.
Minnows swim past our planted feet.

# From the Outermost Island

The stretch of beach she's come to
think of as her own,

the view, cresting the dune,
of the gladdening bay.

\*

How this arm stretches out into the Atlantic,
velvet peninsula, exotic in its lack of lights
when seen at night by plane,

how it eludes the mainland,
but how far short it falls
before its neighbors to the north,
Meat Cove in Nova Scotia, Newfoundland.

And always at its back, the city,
seaboard, whole connected country.

\*

In Starr Carr, northeastern England, archeologists uncovered
an eleven-thousand-year-old house yesterday,
a round house, thatched roof, looking over
a lake. Eleven thousand years ago, when island was connected
to continent. Six thousand years before Stonehenge.

Looking over a lake.

\*

Canoe, kayak, pleasure-boat,
sailboat, schooner, submarine,
steamship, airship, blimp, aeroplane,
space shuttle, hot air balloon, hang-
glider—so many ways to elude gravity,
momentarily.

*

Gravity is not a force of nature,
but the expression of differences
in entropy, a scientist has proposed.
We stand because we are capable
of organizing our information.
What's dead or inanimate is unable
to organize its information sufficiently,
and so it falls or disintegrates or de-
composes. Out of these materials we build.

*

*Then the officials shall address the troops,*
*as follows, Is there anyone who has built a new house*
*but has not dedicated it? Let him go back to his home,*
*lest he die in battle and another dedicate it.*

*

Let her go back to her home. It is not so distinguished
by the rectitude of its carpenters. But it has views
of roofs, and cranes, and tankers in the channel,
this dormer in the wind, her pilothouse.

# Inverted Pendulum

Inclined
as we are
to dwell
as in to be led
astray
to tarry to delay
or even to inhabit
heavy feeling
unevenly
without occasion
some days
a walk
up hill
a leaning to-
ward will set us
straight.

# Bread and Flowers

Besides the big projects
there are the people
who sustain us
nurse us
back to ourselves
who welcome us home
with bread
and flowers,
who wash our hair
when we can't
who tell us distant
sons and daughters
don't worry it's fine
and leave for work even earlier
to deliver mail
and change bandages.
They respond to the ringing phone
by picking it up.
I paint pictures
of the same door
over and over trying
to get it right,
and they
walk through it.
Your life is like
a house without doors,
someone said to my friend,
and she repeats it
to herself
as a reproach.
It is praise.

# A Year in New England

It takes muscle to fillet the bluefish
with an old kitchen knife and the bluefish feels
nothing. The cotton fibers of a t-shirt drink
the indigo except in spectral rings where the cloth
is bound with rubber bands and will not dye.
Dipped in navy, this day, and the deck planks gray
with dots of red from the bluefish blood.
Clams from the pond in an orange metal bowl.

*

Walking after work, the words recede,
only codes of movement, stepping aside and passing,
and being passed. Returning home the air holding
its breath, the light a Russian Wanderer's,
*After a Rainfall*, uninhabited, yet alive.
A backdrop for the staging of itself.
Yellow coldness, puddles in the mud.
The brush of winter waiting for the sky to dry.

*

Sunrise and sea smoke curling off the water.
Eight AM the cannon blast, its echo congruent
with clouds escaping from the cooling towers.
Last night we saw the rings of Saturn, fused by distance
into one wide white band circling the star. A tiny icon
like a lunula, drawn near to earth. And soon the harbor frozen,
the tide a feathered surface, buoys bound and bells held fast.
Channels cut by coast guard for the ferries thick with birds.

*

This morning when I woke I felt alive,
a feeling slow and sure as snowdrops. "When the sap begins to flow,"
Thoreau wrote in April, "our diseases become more violent.
It is now advancing toward summer apace, and we seem to be reserved
to taste its sweetness, but to perform what great deeds?
Do we detect the reason why we also did not die?"

# Interior

There'll always be things to grumble about

but not today, not while the trees still wear their leaves,

late leaves, green and patient in the sun.

Only the brittle few on the front steps

and dun-colored needles blanketing

the beds remind me that it's fall just the same.

Late October, so the mailman has to reach

his hand through gauzy webbing to the gate latch,

duck past skeletons and witches dangling from boughs.

These houses must have children or time on hand.

Last night as we drove home from the birthday,

the moon was stuck in traffic till we moved,

and then it grew entangled in the trees.

I'll take Daddy's axe and chop them down!

my daughter said. Husbandry not being what it was,

the axe sounds like a cipher or make believe,

but we keep one in the basement, the sharp edge

covered. Soon it will be time

for the city and yellow buses to carry home the grown

and small passengers dismissed for the day.

For now, the baby, awake and uncomplaining,

studies the ceiling as I type, the afternoon so quiet,

the keys must sound to him like the whole world.

# This Republic

Deep winter. The closet doors that stayed shut
in summer now ajar, in the half-dark
blue, pink, white, pink shirtsleeves blooming.
The bulbs I forced have lost their scent,
yellowing into a tall old age, tall and unobtrusive,
and more palmlike than paperwhite.

A paperwhite without its perfume is like the intellect,
straining upward, knotty, gnarled, stewing in coffee-
colored waters, its leaves—if one can call them that—akimbo,
sometimes forcibly staked so as not to fall over,
staked through the heart of the plant, which is the bulb,
from which spring's fresh fetid smell once sprang.

Laundry dried, folded and hung.
The baby baptized before its six-month birthday.
Last night the first snow,
the season defined now.

Always the concupiscent edging out the intellect,
and the irascible saying it should be so.

# Nowhere

Where's nowhere?
    she asked

I had no answer
    until bed the roof

creaked overhead I thought
    of those without

and sleep upon them too
    light of the stars

a cold refusal
    nowhere

distant borough
    home

to nobody
    to many.

# At the A.R.T.

Or on the terrace, anyway,
I'm drinking iced tea, watching
as the set is staged,
a banquet on the lawn below
among the bright perennials, their beds
just edged. Such fuss over the chowder,
how to keep it hot
while other hands set up the bar,
the folding tables, crimson cloth,
the rows of stemware, bottles.
Small letters on a placard staked
in gravel by the drive: PRIVATE
RESIDENCE. Is the hostess upstairs,
dressing? Can she see across the street
the man with long hair, just like mine
perched on the post & beam
the man whose home has been this street,
this square, as long as I remember,
likely longer? The look of a thru-hiker
but he's here for good.
The mountain of white napkins
grows, the girls talk while they fold,
the boys bring steaming pitchers,
pour them into silver trays,
and seal with lids the heat inside.
Outside the cook tent, milling cooks,
the head chef's phone is dead,
he's asking for the time
and it is close
this evening, early June,
high pressure having cleared the air,

a low sun working still
and warm along my arms, my shins.
Sitting on this wall beside the hostas,
shade-lovers, sheltered by my shadow,
incognizant of our good luck.

# Reverie

After the vernal equinox until the end of August there is room

to sit together in the red womb chair and reread before breakfast

the books I brought to this island you will leave.


No matter that you've upset the boat again,

there will always be time for tea and a walk across the fields.

You will be asked back another day.


Sitting quiet against a rock and feeling the sun on your fur

might not look like foraging but come the days of scarcity and cold

and you'll feed others, the whole mischief, with seeds of color.


And maybe you're a single dam with lots of kits,

hopping and fetching, feeding and wiping, sweeping and teaching,

one day you'll gather your litter together and tell them,

now the time has come to have some fun.

And despite your years and country origins,

you'll outrun the vested jackrabbits.

The gold shoes will remind you.

And who will be left to pull out my chair?

# Talking Cure

*for J.W.L.*

During the lecture on *The Rite of Spring* I studied the pruning of the cherry trees.

A coincidence of seasons.

I was fond of lecturing my mother there are lots of ways to be.

Faced with a brick wall Brodsky writes which way to go.

The word for crossroads the same as the word for road, the word for journey.

There are no roundabouts in my mother tongue.

Say you heard a knock on your door at night, it was likely the black car running so best be packed and your poems safe with an amanuensis.

The Russian sentence was to isolate but preserve. Disappeared in Argentina, struggled against in China.

Usually your nearest neighbor.

Say you found some snapshots in the book he lent you, they could be his nieces, right?

When we misplaced the child he was up the hill eating blackberries as we joked.

Doesn't everyone learn not to touch a prickly pear by touching one?

How to explain what I remember best after twenty years is you on the
  rocks, saying into the wind, sometimes the wind makes me think I'll
  lose my mind.

# Liminal

That ordinary afternoon
I saw you clearly,
  though the days since you were born
  and not beside me fewer than my fingers,

nearly five years, like hiking hours in the mountains,
granite crags then suddenly
  an alpine bloom. Was it a minute?
  Maybe less I watched you

bring the watermelon to your lips
and delicate, you split the fruit in two.
  The soft planes of your face
  in perfect focus startled me

into attention while you gazed
beyond, alert, absorbed, unclouded
  as the day and seemed to grow
  composed of cream

and primrose, jade in shadow, chestnut.
All those nights necessity caressed
  your brow so that I might
  conspire with the air,

my sight as mild and impartial
as the light against your cheek, the filaments
  of glinting hair uplifted, till you turned
  to me and smiling, spoke.

# Gammon

Looking up, "The purple now," she dips
her brush and finishes the day. The flag

descends. She draws the fire with a marker
on fax paper uncurling from its spool.

Inventory of glasses, the handblown ones
blue-edged could hold a sunset neat, the new

regime is softball-sized and etched with tigers.
In town they're pulling draughts for every swinging

door. Don't get angry, don't get angry.
The soaker's washed and left to dry. Iron

Hessians oversee the fire gone
to bed beside the harbor, geese calling

each to each triangulate the dark.
Passing through or are they wintering over?

In chevron resolve. Like waking to
the rain and walking anyway. She

thinking of what to do with pawpaw jelly,
he of mildew and of marrow, while

their youngest bouncing gums the leather
dice cup, sister rolls, counts, and makes

a point. Get even says the horizon
like the sun, democratic and unsparing.

# Marathon

Only the moon over Soldier's Field Road sees us depart,
quiet until the sun apocalyptic above the hospital
jars us into words at river's bend, electric pink
feedback feathering the water, mercury rising.
Last time I saw the sunrise I gave birth. Only the fittest
they've said should run and you're among them. Human
technicolor snakes and schoolbuses perambulate
the park and idly limber in preparation to go west
while in the garden an old man bends his knees and pushes air
with just his hands, slow as spring. The swan boats
out of hibernation sway, chained to the dock,
and a gray-skirted sneakered lady speedwalks through it all.
One day I'll wake this early of my own accord
and imagine where I'll go and meet me there.

# The Forest Next Door

Having discovered it
    when she forgot to draw
        the nursery curtains

he trains his blue eyes
    on the pines
        and having no words

he chortles
    and having no horse
        he rocks himself

not to sleep
    but forward fixedly
        toward stepped and verdant cliffs

this small explorer
    of deep grasping
        fastening

the solid surfaces each
    to each until the dimming
        relinquishes

the light and him.
    The forest breathes,
        the oceans leap,

over mapped continents, blue reaching
over green for blue,
the cartographer's view

then a marble, swaddled
by clouds it seems, small earth
of given names once dreamed.

## ACKNOWLEDGMENTS

I am grateful to the MacDowell Colony for its support in the completion of this book.

Thank you to all the editors in whose pages the following poems first appeared. "In the Shadows," "This Republic," and "Requiem for the Stars" first appeared in *The Yale Review*; "Seeking Even the Smallest of Signs" and "Gammon" first appeared in *Poetry*; "The Color of Nostalgia" first appeared in *The Harvard Review Online*; "Fair Sun" first appeared in *The Harvard Review* and was chosen for *Poetry Daily*; "How Should We Live Our Lives" first appeared in *The Hudson Review*; "Dyer Pond" first appeared in *The Antioch Review*; "Look Out for Hope" and "How Things Speak Then Pass" first appeared in *Raritan*; "From the Outermost Island" and "Failed Sublime" first appeared in *236*. And thank you to Sally Taylor for commissioning "Attachment" for *Consenses*, a multigenre art installation which opened in West Tisbury, MA, in 2014.

I am indebted to my family, friends, and teachers; to Etel Adnan for kindly granting me the use of her painting on the book cover; to Chelsea Bingham, Michael Russem, Sue Ramin, and especially, David Godine; and for everything and always, to Philip Walsh and Lillian and Philip.

"To Know Wisdom and Instruction": The phrase is from Proverbs 1:2, and also the first words written in the Armenian alphabet in 405 AD.

"Le Palais Idéal": The postman Cheval is Ferdinand Cheval (1836–1924).

"Attachment": The italicized lines are by the Portuguese poet Fernando Pessoa (1888–1935).

"Andranik": Andranik is Andranik Vartanian, my grandfather. He was a boy living in the eastern province of Muş (one of the earliest centers of historic Armenia), within the Ottoman Empire, when the mass killings began in 1915; he was the only member of his family to survive the Armenian genocide. "Andranik" is a narrative poem based on his testimony.

"Elective Affinities" is in memory of Svetlana Boym.

"From the Outermost Island": The italicized lines are from Deuteronomy, by way of Tracy Kidder.

Susan Barba's poems have appeared in *Poetry*, *Raritan*, *The Yale Review*, *The Hudson Review*, *The Antioch Review*, *Harvard Review*, and *Poetry Daily*. She has received fellowships from the MacDowell Colony and Yaddo. She is a senior editor with New York Review Books.